Ideas

NOTES

Canadian representatives: General Publishing Co., Ltd.,
30 Lesmill Road, Don Mills, Ontario M3B 2T6.

9 8 7 6 5 4 3 2
Digit on the right indicates the number of this printing.

ISBN 1–56138–646–4

Cover design by Toby Schmidt
Interior design by Susan E. Van Horn
Edited by Brian Perrin
Printed in the United States

This book may be ordered by mail from the publisher.
Please add $1.00 for postage and handling.
But try your bookstore first!

Running Press Book Publishers
125 South Twenty-second Street
Philadelphia, Pennsylvania 19103–4399

Ideas

NOTES

RUNNING PRESS
PHILADELPHIA · LONDON

Individual ideas—like—breaths—are waiting

to be drawn from unlimited supply.

Margaret Danner (1915–1988)
American poet

Good ideas are like radio waves; they're all around us, there for the grabbing. All you have to do is tune them in.

Joel Saltzman
20th-century American writer

Ideas may come at any time.

B. B. KING (B. 1925)
AMERICAN SINGER-SONGWRITER

*The human mind, once stretched
to a new idea, never goes back to its
original dimensions.*

Oliver Wendell Holmes, Sr. (1809–1894)
American physician, educator, poet, and writer

When I come upon some idea that
is not of this world, I feel as though
this world had grown wider.

Antonio Porchia (1886–1968)
Italian-born Argentinean writer

*A*bove all, remember that the most
important thing you can take anywhere
is not a Gucci bag or French-cut jeans;
it's an open mind.

GAIL RUBIN BERENY (B. 1942)
AMERICAN DIRECTOR, PRODUCER, AND WRITER

Imagination is the beginning of creation. You imagine what you desire;

you will what you imagine; and at last you create what you will.

George Bernard Shaw (1856–1950)
Irish playwright and writer

$\mathcal{R}$everies, wild reveries, lead our lives.

Gaston Bachelard (1884–1962)
French writer

We become what we dream. . . .

We achieve in reality, in substance,

only the pictures of the imagination.

LAWRENCE DURRELL (1912–1990)
FRENCH-BORN ENGLISH WRITER

You must never think that your most recent idea is your best or your last. You must be willing to keep searching your imagination and intuition for new versions and variations of that idea.

Bill Moyers (b. 1934)
American journalist

... remember that Thomas Edison

found over two thousand ways not

to make a light bulb.

Tom Wujec
20th-century American writer

And how do these creative thoughts come? They come in a slow way. It is the little bomb of revelation bursting inside you. I found I never took a long, solitary walk without some of these silent, little inward bombs bursting quietly: "I see. I understand that now!" and a feeling of happiness.

BRENDA UELAND (1891–1985)
AMERICAN EDUCATOR, EDITOR, AND WRITER

*Often it is the most irrelevant objects
that are capable of stimulating the
mind towards a new idea.*

Edward De Bono (b. 1933)
English writer

*E*verybody has a lot of knowledge;
by shifting the contexts in which you
think about it, you'll discover new ideas.

Roger von Oech
20th-century American writer

How many times it thundered before Franklin took the hint! How many apples fell on Newton's head before he took the hint! Nature is always hinting at us.

ROBERT FROST (1874–1963)
AMERICAN POET

Inspiration is disturbing. She does not believe in guarantees or insurance or strict schedules. . . . She will be there when you need her but you have to take it on trust. Surrender. She knows when you need her better than you do.

J. Ruth Gendler
20th-century American writer

Ideas? They should come to you from everywhere: a face, a voice, a remark, a news item, a building, an empty road, a deserted street, someone hurrying, a dog barking in the night.

ELISABETH OGILVIE (B. 1917)
AMERICAN WRITER

Thoughts just arise impersonally from the bottom of our minds. That is the nature of mind—it creates thoughts.

Natalie Goldberg
20th-century American writer

Someone has said that an idea has some of the mysterious quality of an atoll or island that suddenly appears in a spot where ancient charts showed nothing but deep blue sea. Mysterious? Not if you think of the countless, unseen coral builders working below the surface of the sea. Not if you think of an idea being the final result of a long series of unseen idea-building processes which go on beneath the surface of the conscious mind.

Jeannette Eyerly (b. 1908)
American writer

It's all out there, floating free, waiting for you to pull it down and anchor it.

ANNE BERNAYS (B. 1930)
AMERICAN WRITER

*Nothing is more exhilarating than
the discovery that a complex pattern has
lain in your mind ready to unfold.*

Janet Burroway (b. 1936)
American writer

I think I am more interested in the movement among ideas than in the ideas themselves, the way one goes from one point to another rather than the destination or the origin.

John Ashbery (b. 1927)
American writer

Ideas will set each other off like firecrackers in a bunch. It is simply a matter of somehow igniting the first of them. From then on, things take care of themselves.

RICHARD ARMOUR (1906–1989)
AMERICAN EDUCATOR AND WRITER

Heady, wild and totally outrageous ideas can be brought into line, maybe only momentarily, before they are banished as unrealistic. It is the season for minds sharp as blades—agile and springing from one extravagant thought to another.

Mirabel Osler
20th-century English writer

. . . even under the best conditions
it takes time to develop an idea and
even more time to create art.

Anne Grant
20th-century American writer

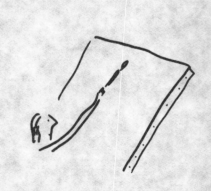

Guard your tongue in your mouth, and in age you may mature a thought that will be of service to your people.

NATIVE AMERICAN (SIOUX) PROVERB

Creative will is patience.

Marina Tsvetayeva (1892–1941)
Russian poet and writer

*A*n idea, like a ghost . . . must be spoken

to a little before it will explain itself.

Charles Dickens (1812–1870)
English writer

It is something that grows painstakingly, a bit at a time, often through periods of despair and drought. Yet there are moments when miracles do happen and something comes clear in an instant—though not as a rule the whole thing.

PHYLLIS WHITNEY (B. 1903)
AMERICAN WRITER

With luck, talent, and studiousness, one manages to make a little pearl, or egg, or something. . . . But what gives birth to it is what happens inside the soul and the mind, . . .

Edna O'Brien (b. 1936)
Irish writer

. . . cultivate a habit of mind that provides

fertile soil for ideas to burrow into.

Jane Adams (b. 1940)
American writer

Ideas often flash across our minds more complete

than we could make them after much labor.

FRANÇOIS DE LA ROCHEFOUCAULD (1613–1680)
FRENCH MORALIST

Development of ideas — that's where the diamonds are. The difference between dirt and ore is what you can get out of it.

Frank Herbert (1920–1986)
American writer

. . . creativity is dangerous. We cannot open ourselves to new insight without
endangering the security of our prior assumptions. We cannot propose new ideas
without risking disapproval and rejection. . . . Its pleasure is not the comfort of
the safe harbor, but the thrill of the reaching sail.

Robert Grudin (b. 1938)
American educator and writer

Gradually, the idea became a giant under its own power, and it coaxed, nursed, and drove me. Ideas are like that. First you give life and action and guidance to ideas, then they take on power of their own and sweep aside all opposition.

NAPOLEON HILL (C. 1883–1970)
AMERICAN WRITER

esire applied to an idea is the same as pouring fuel into a powerful engine to keep it running.

Wally Amos
20th-century American entrepreneur

Ideas are the glory of man alone. No other creature can have them. Only man can get a vision and an inspiration that will lift him above the level of himself and send him forth against all opposition.

Mathew Henson (1866–1955)
American explorer

Ideas rise with new morning but never die . . .

only names, places, people change. . . .

FRANK MARSHALL DAVIS (1905–1987)
AMERICAN JOURNALIST AND WRITER

Nothing is stronger than an idea whose time has come.

Victor Hugo (1802–1885)
French poet and writer